EASY PIANO
SONGS FOR KIDS

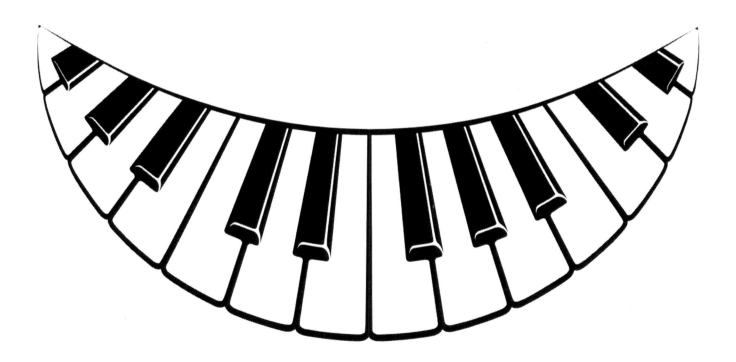

easy-sheet-music.com

Contents

Are You Sleeping?

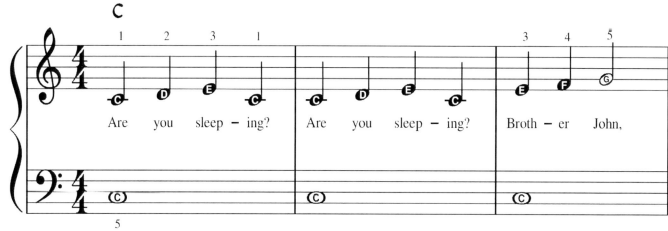

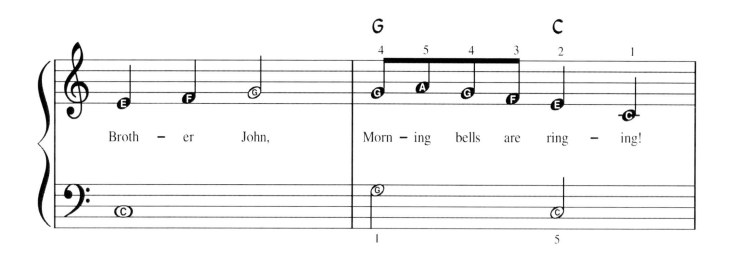

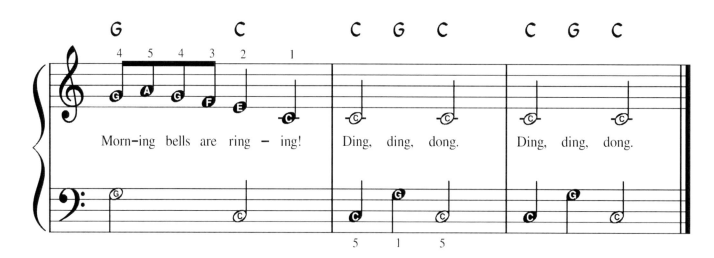

Twinkle Twinkle Little Star

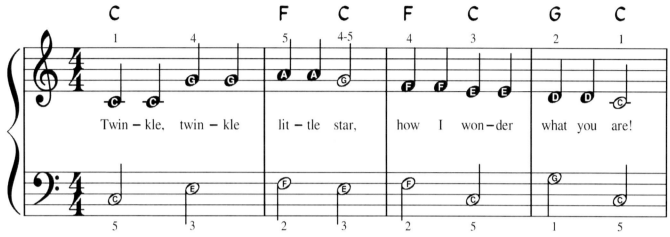

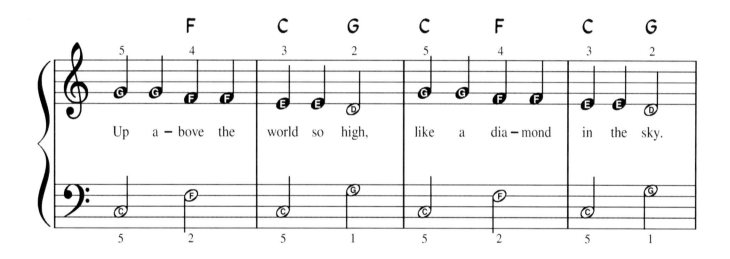

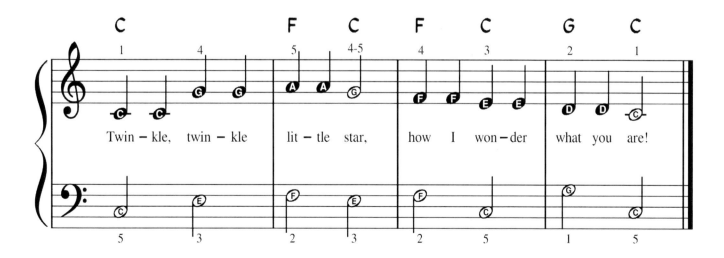

Can Can

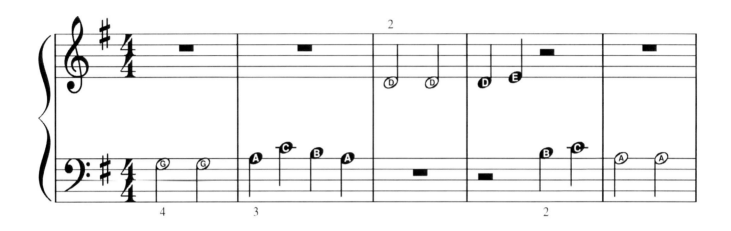

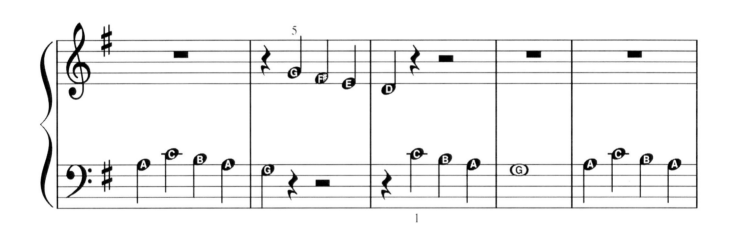

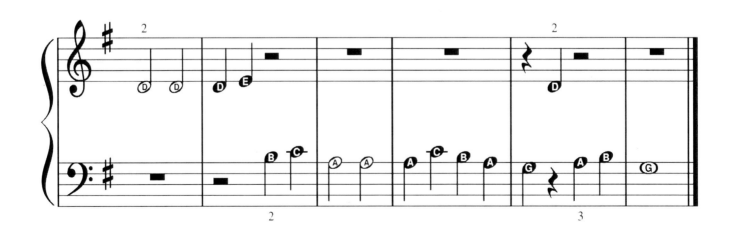

Baa, Baa, Black Sheep

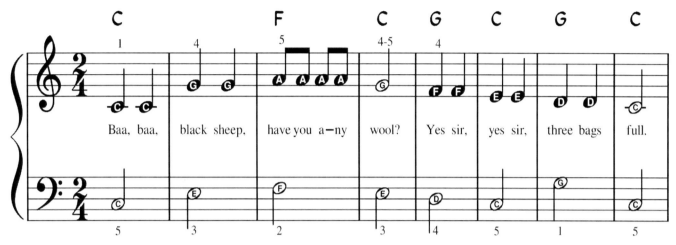

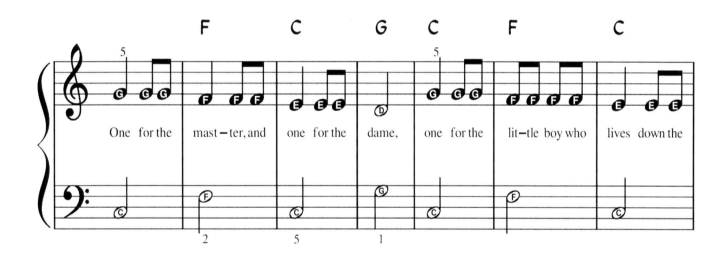

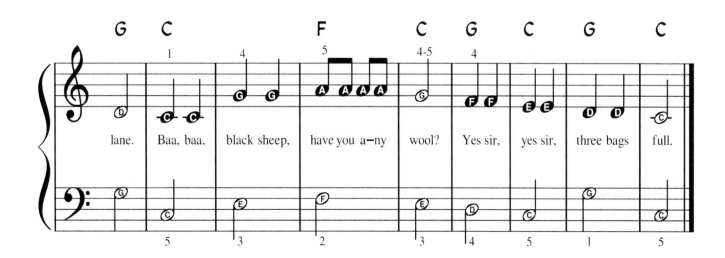

Ode To Joy

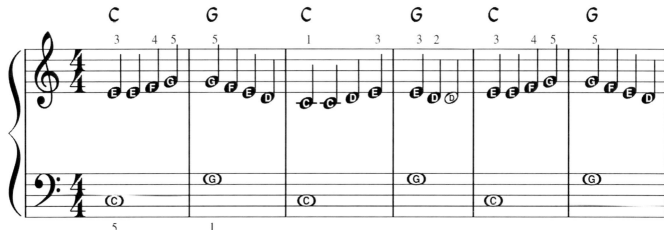

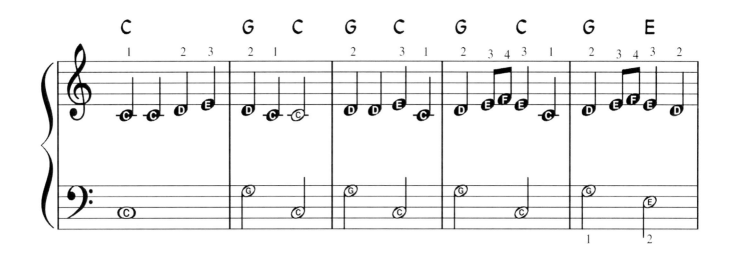

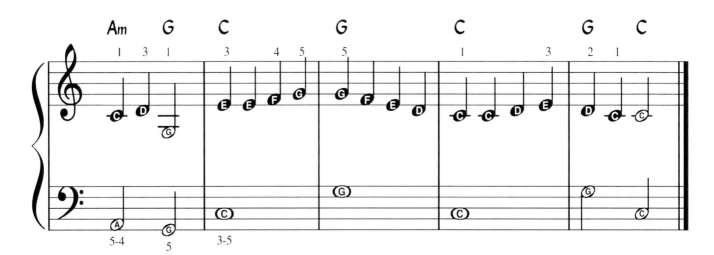

Skip To My Lou

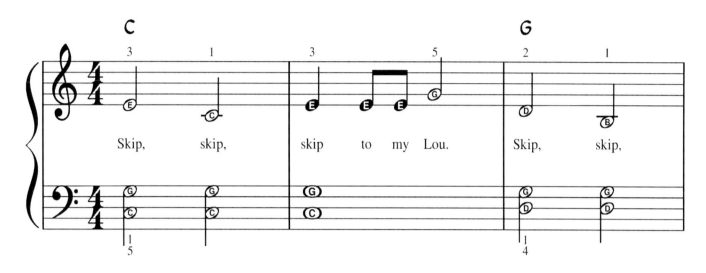

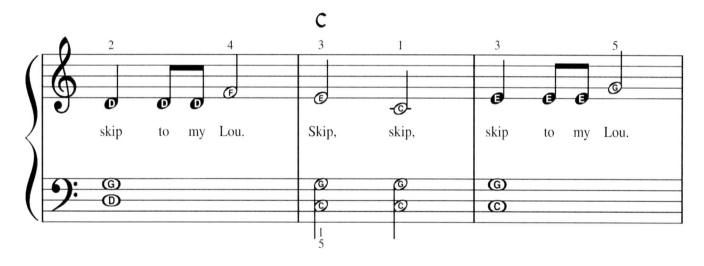

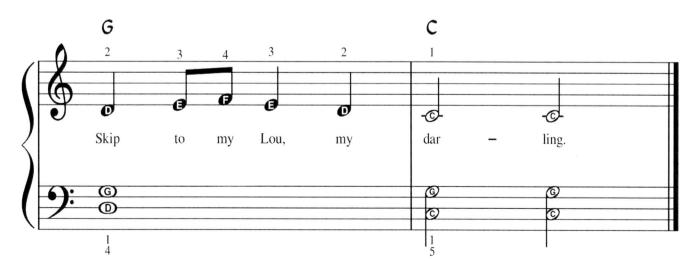

The Mulberry Bush

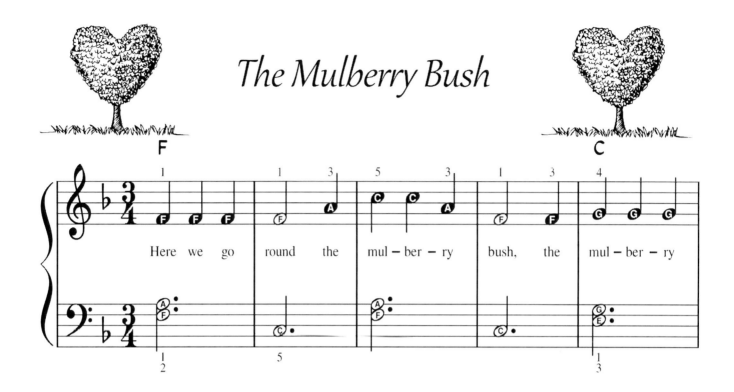

Here we go round the mul — ber — ry bush, the mul — ber — ry

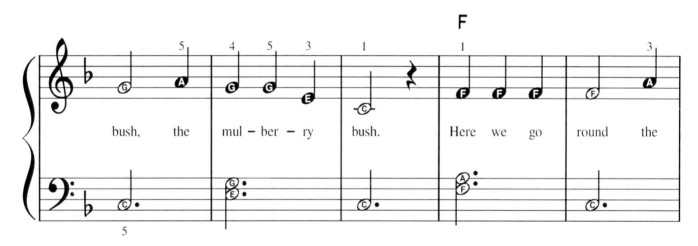

bush, the mul — ber — ry bush. Here we go round the

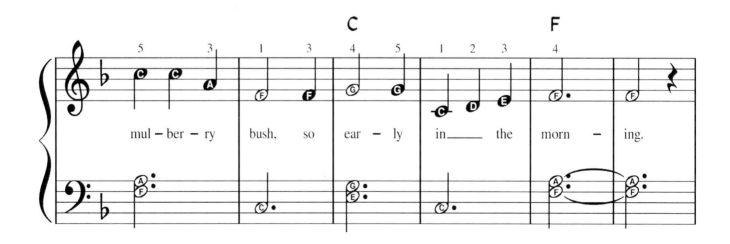

mul — ber — ry bush, so ear — ly in ___ the morn — ing.

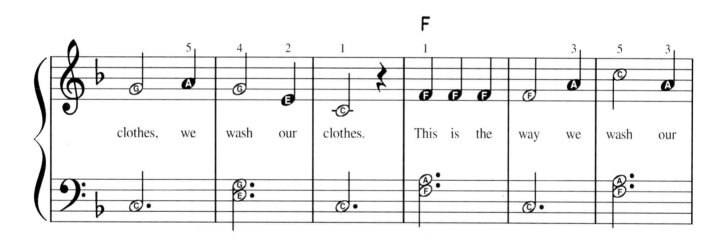

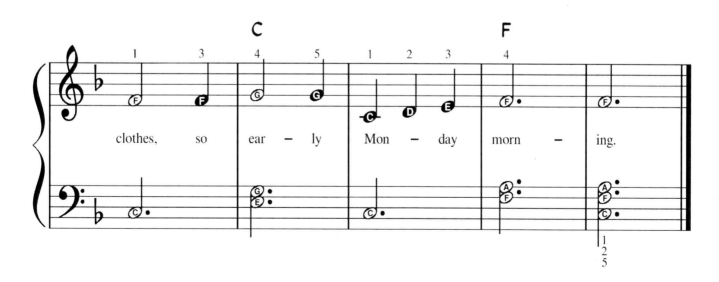

This Old Man

Row, Row, Row Your Boat

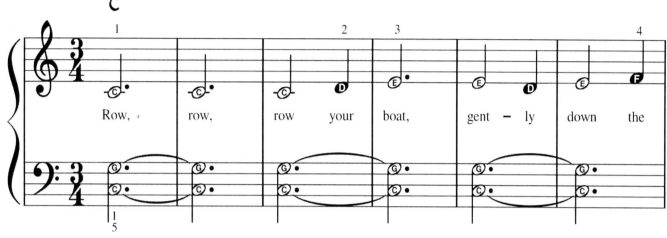

Row, row, row your boat, gent – ly down the

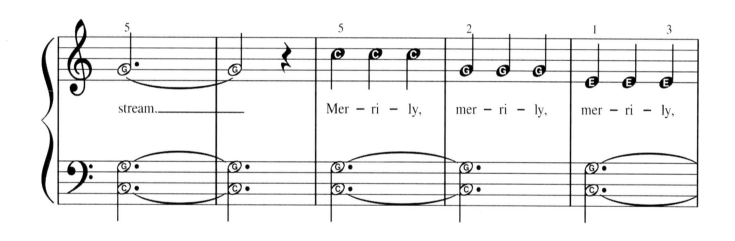

stream. Mer – ri – ly, mer – ri – ly, mer – ri – ly,

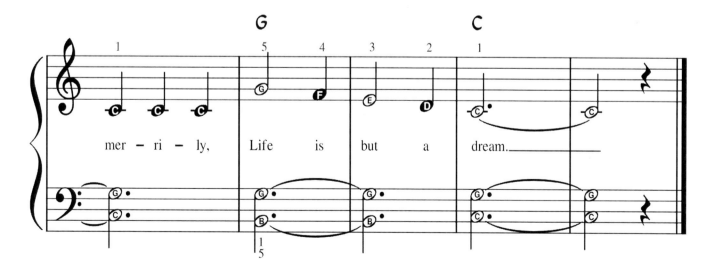

mer – ri – ly, Life is but a dream.

Three Blind Mice

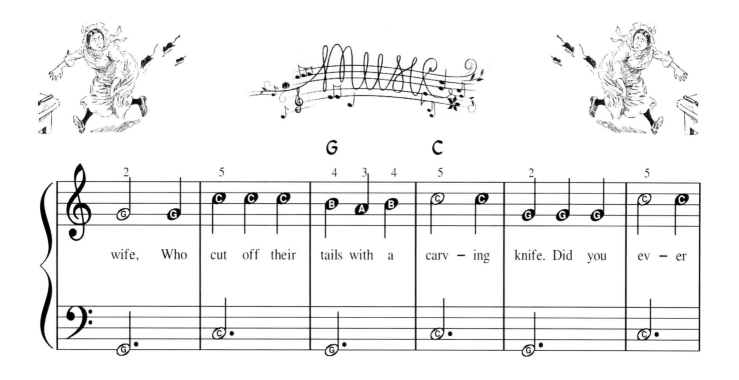

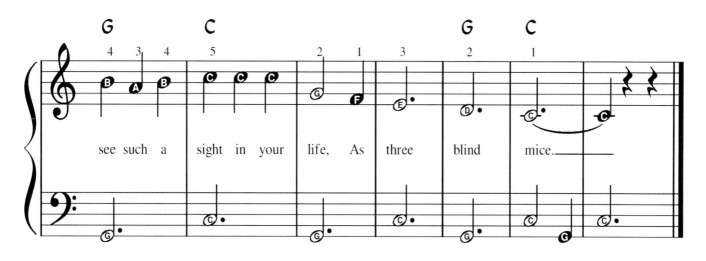

When The Saints Go Marching In

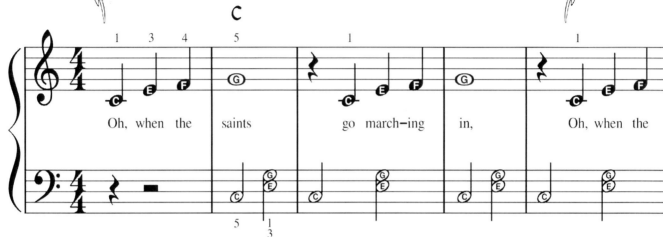

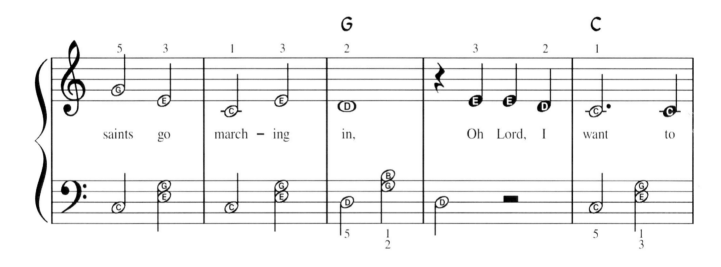

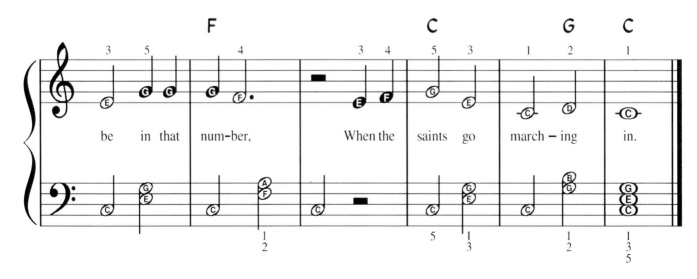

The Grand Old Duke Of York

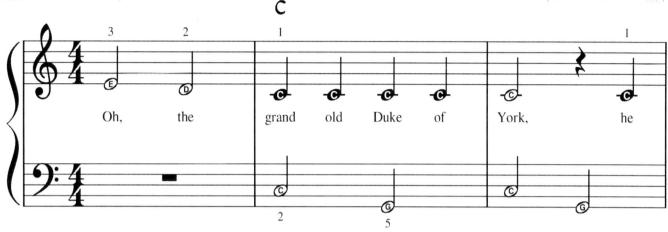

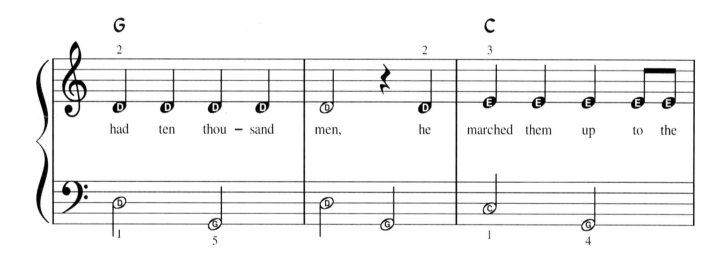

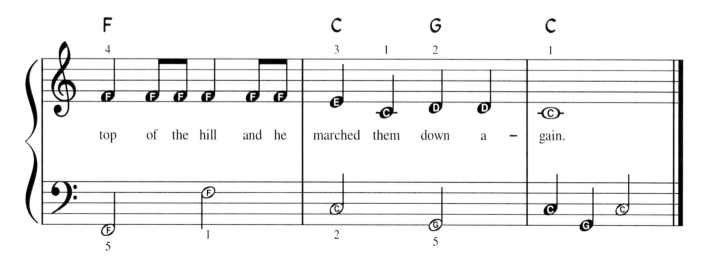

The Muffin Man

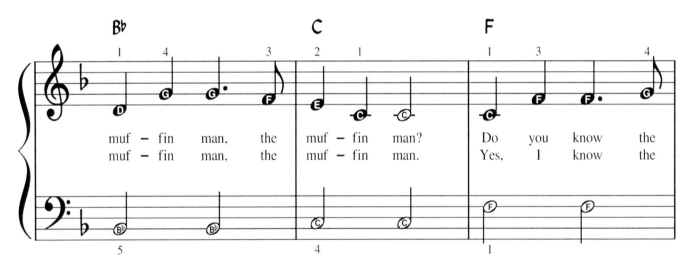

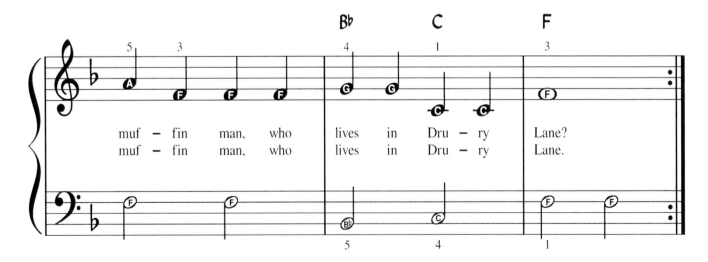

Lavender's Blue

19

Jingle Bells

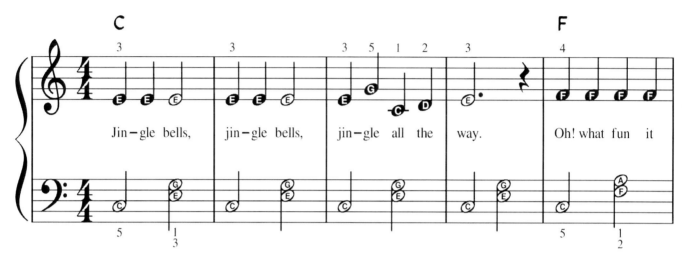

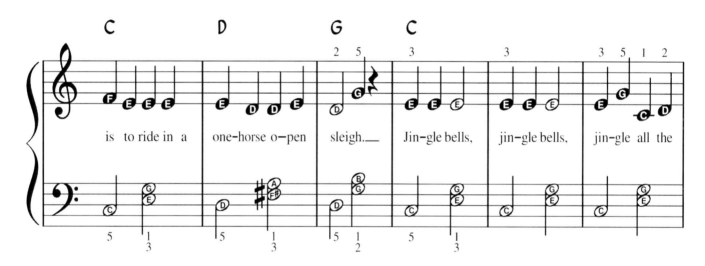

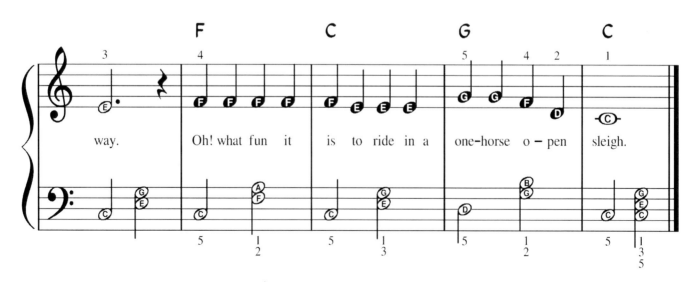

Kum Ba Yah

Alphabet Song

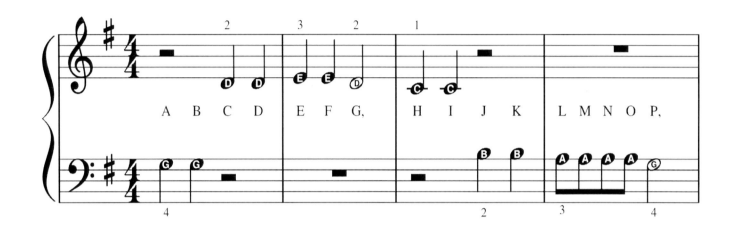

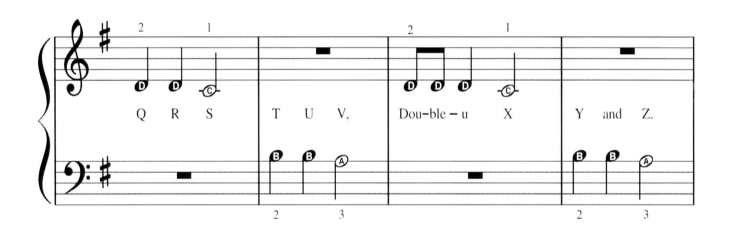

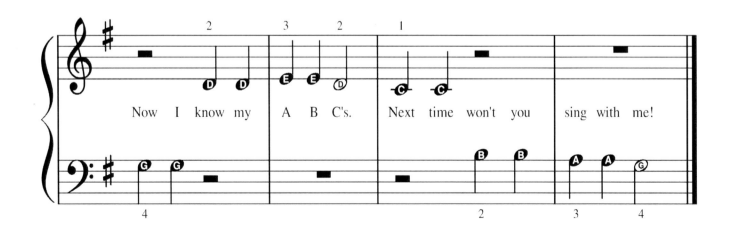

A-Tisket, A-Tasket

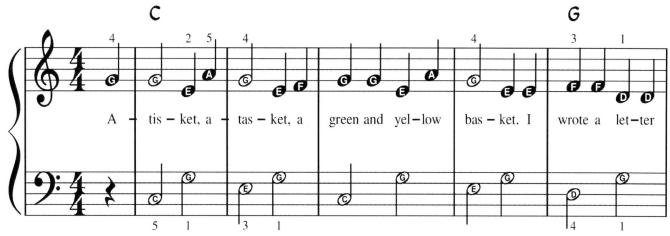

A - tis – ket, a - tas – ket, a | green and yel-low | bas – ket. I | wrote a let–ter

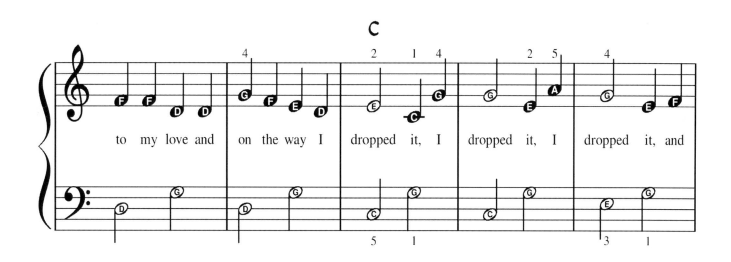

to my love and | on the way I | dropped it, I | dropped it, I | dropped it, and

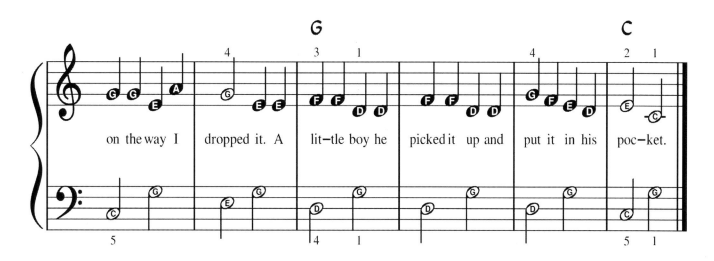

on the way I | dropped it. A | lit–tle boy he | picked it up and | put it in his | poc–ket.

London Bridge

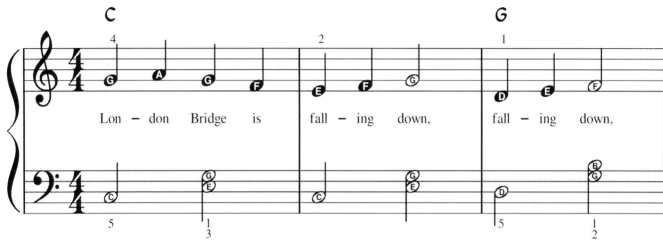

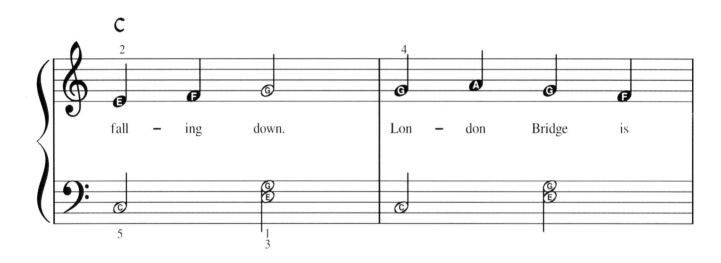

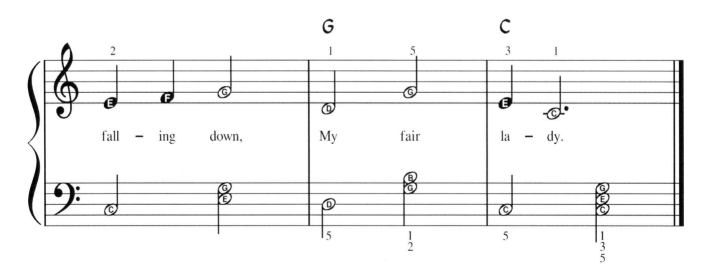

Mary Had a Little Lamb

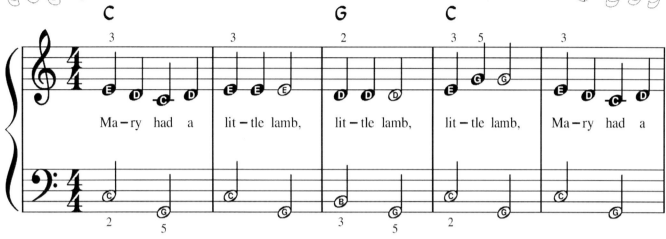

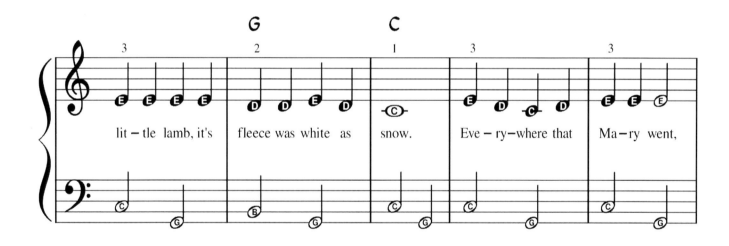

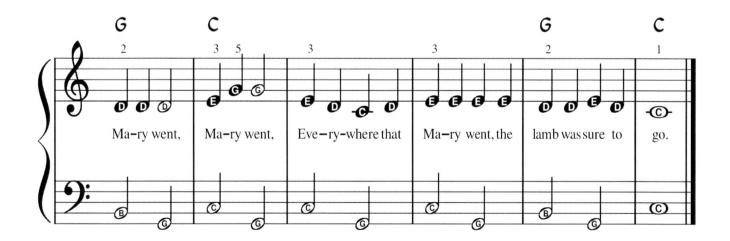

Old MacDonald

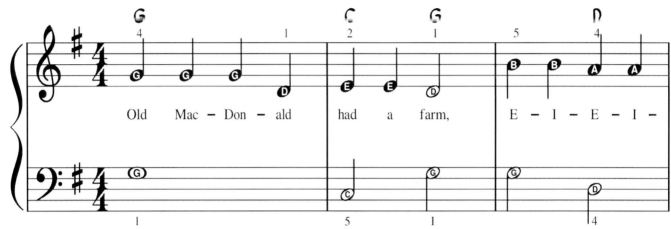

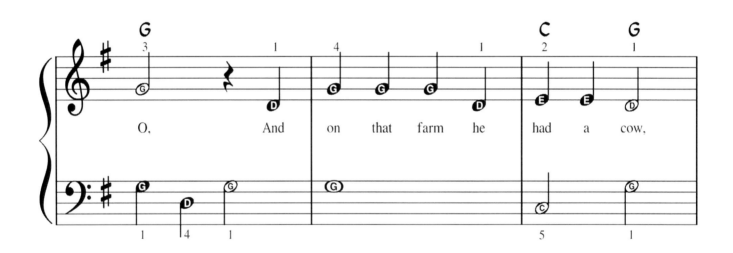

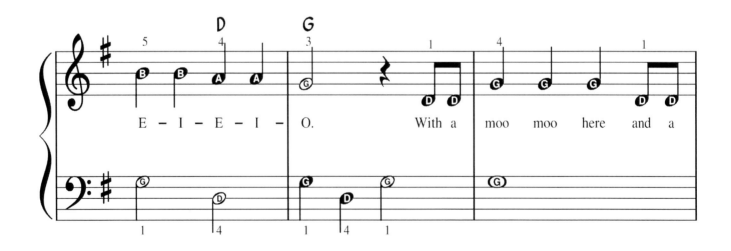

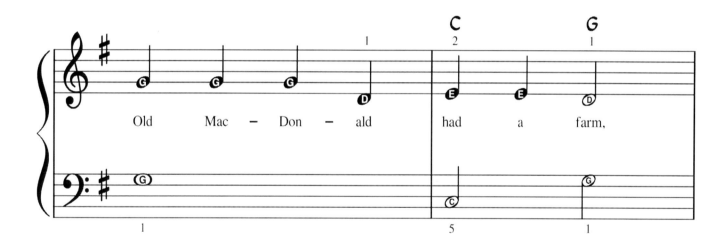

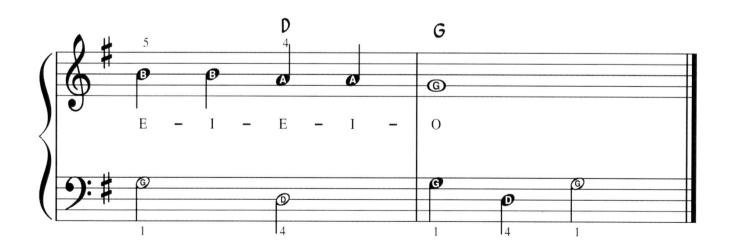

Brahms' Lullaby

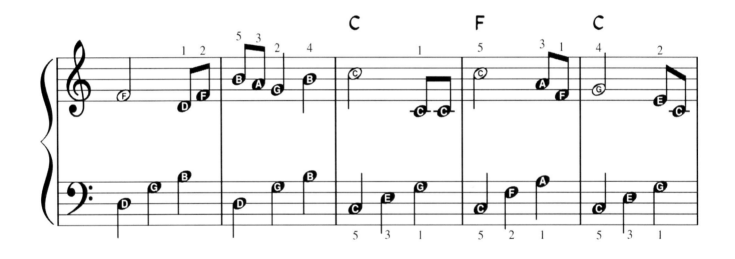

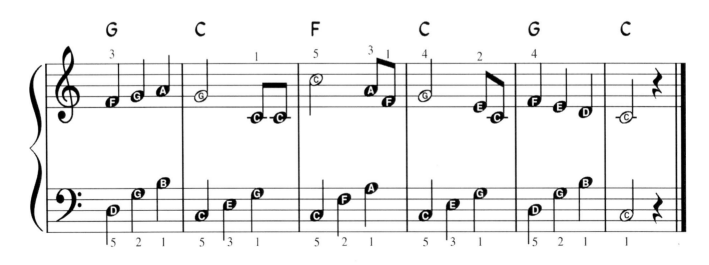

Amazing Grace

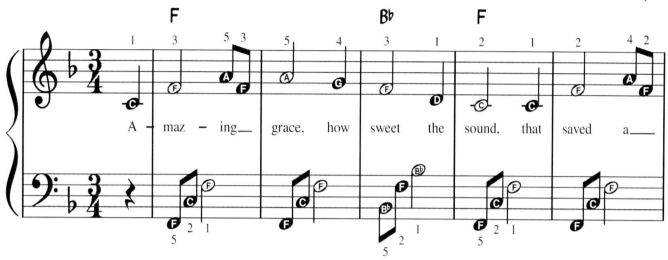

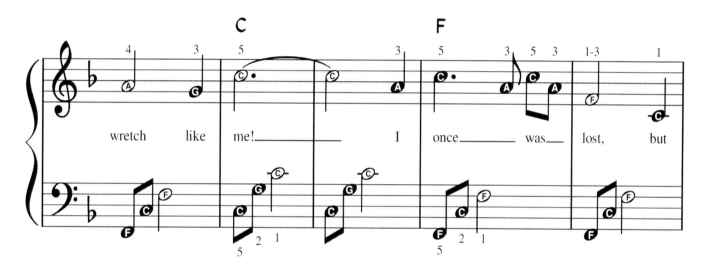

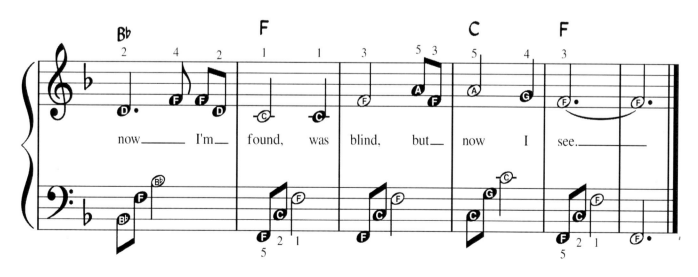

Clementine (Oh, My Darling)

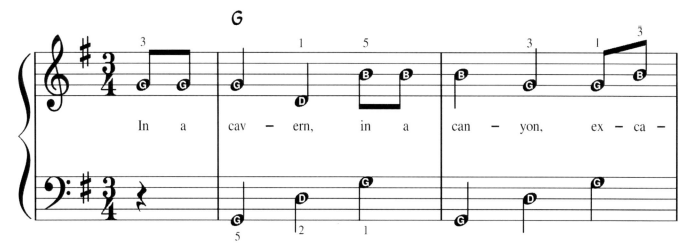

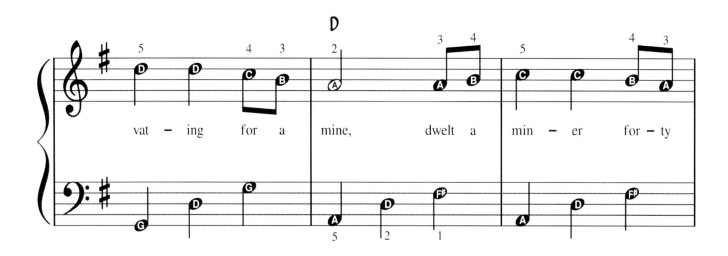

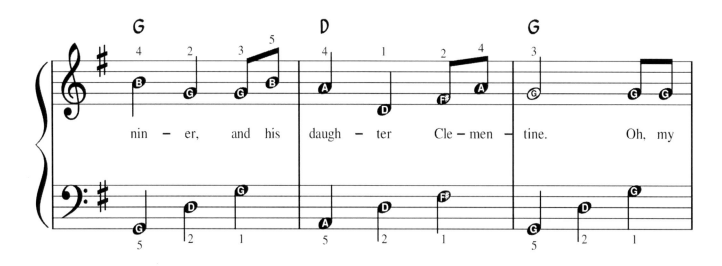

Girls and Boys

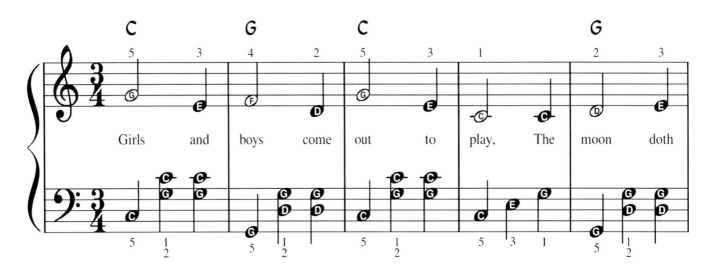

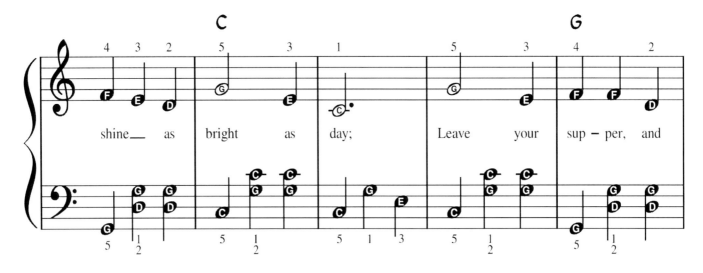

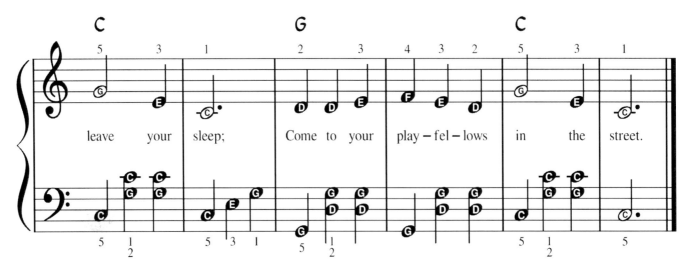

Bingo

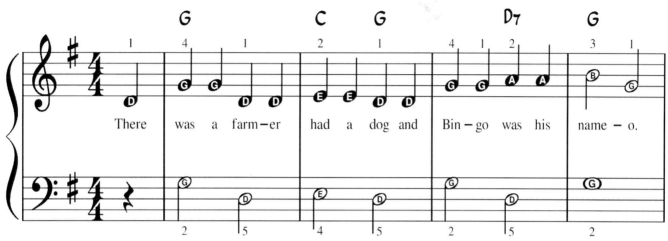

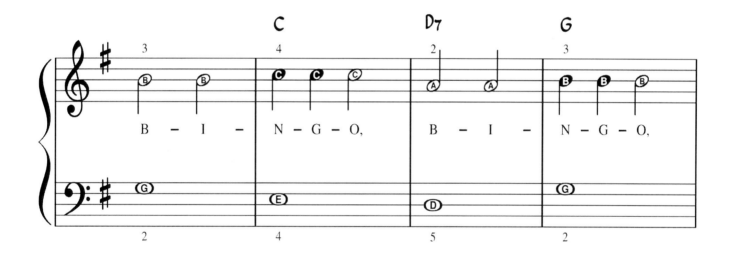

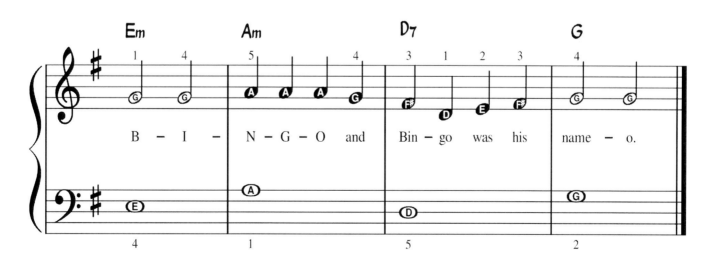

Hickory Dickory Dock

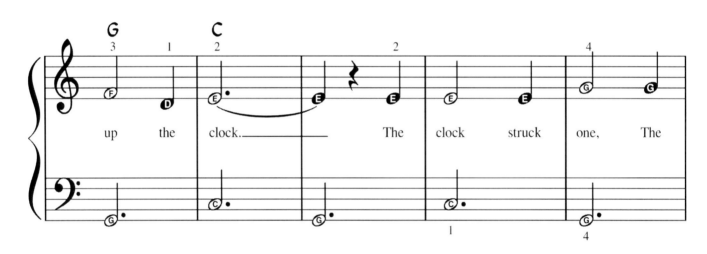

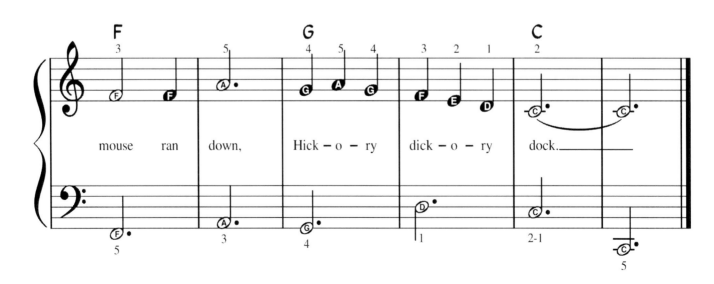

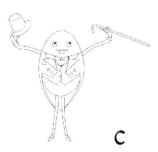

Humpty Dumpty

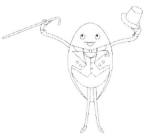

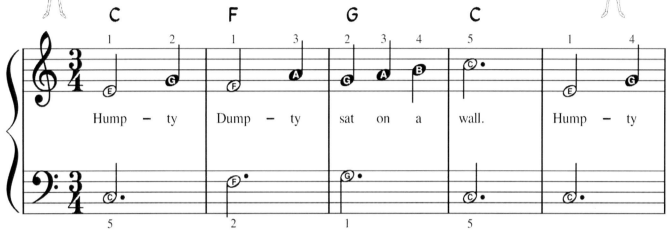

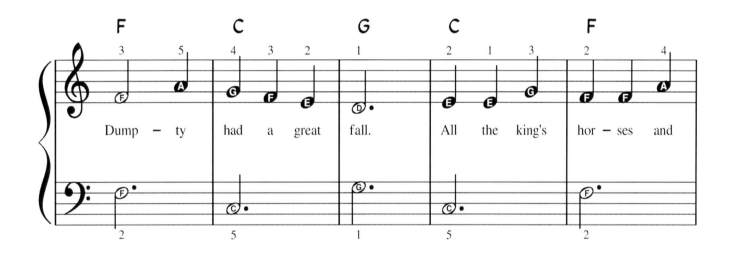

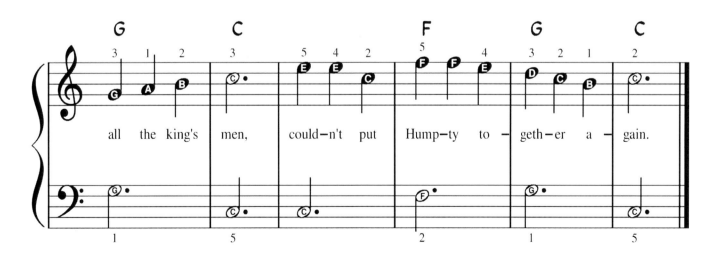

My Bonnie Lies Over The Ocean

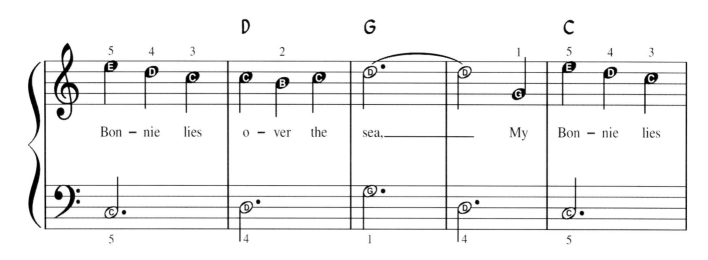

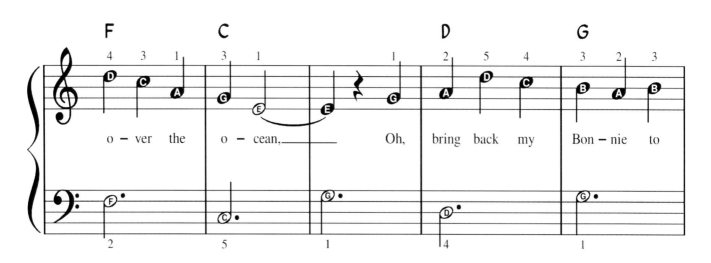

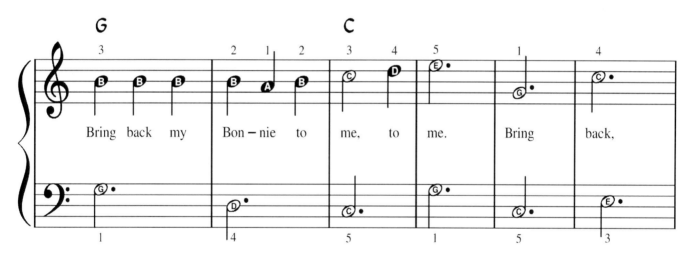

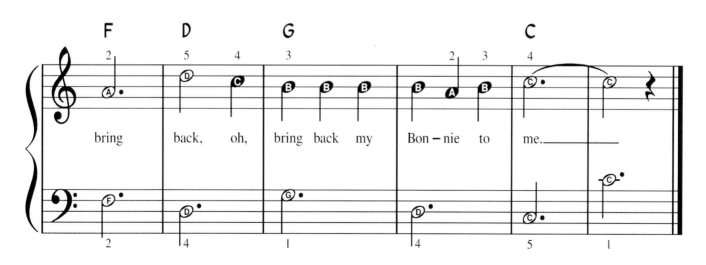

Polly Put The Kettle On

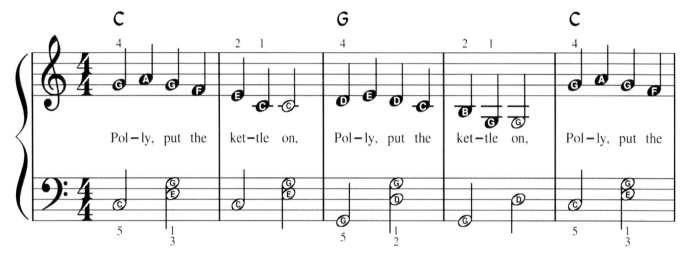

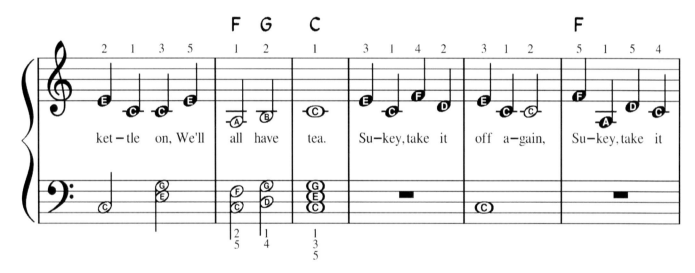

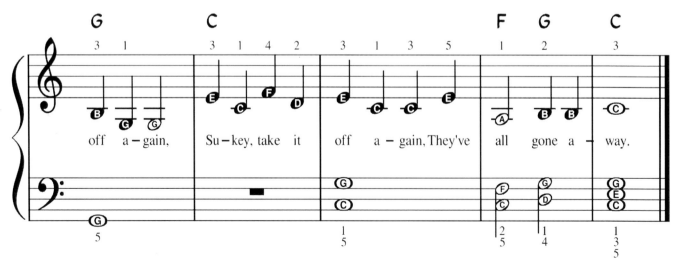

Pop! Goes the Weasel

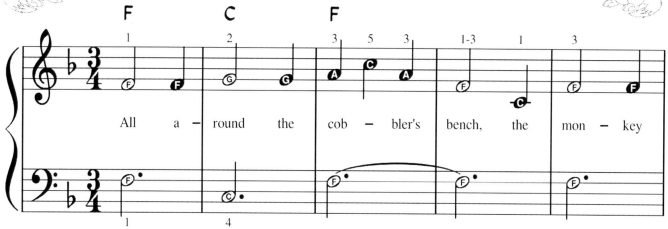

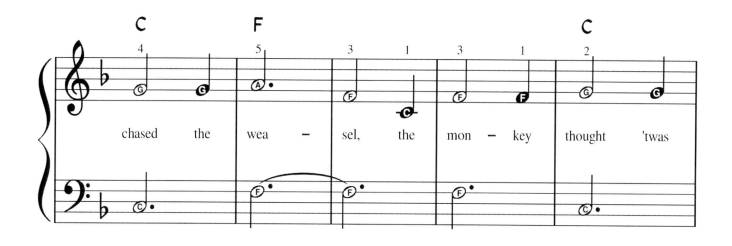

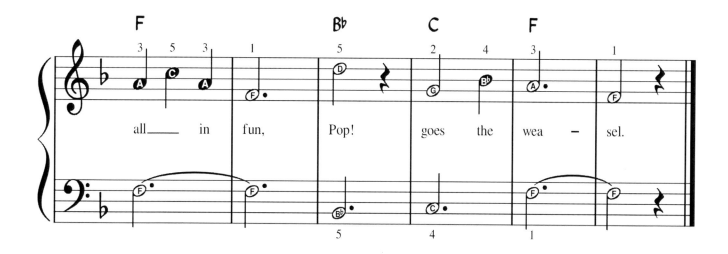

Rock-A-Bye, Baby

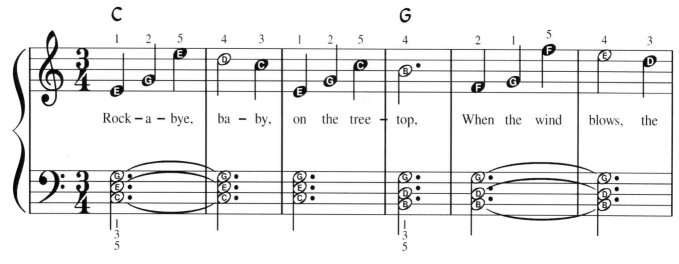

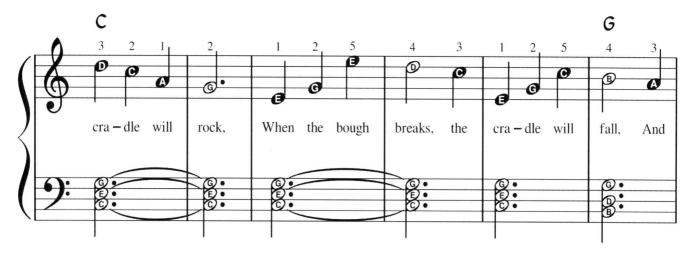

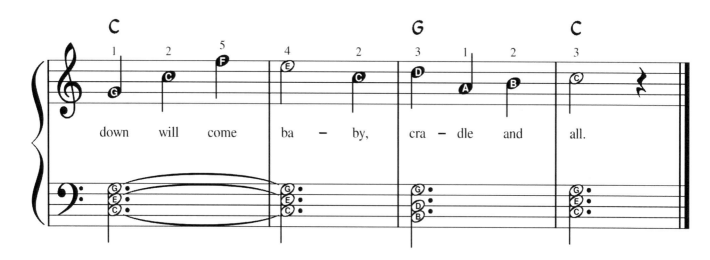

Scarborough Fair

Silent Night

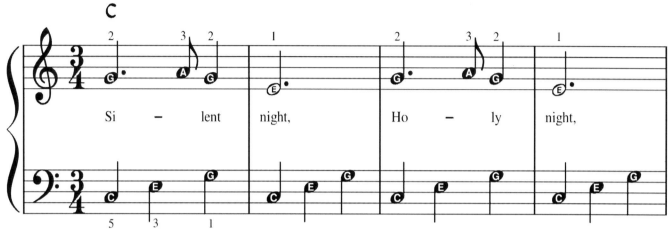

Si – lent night, Ho – ly night,

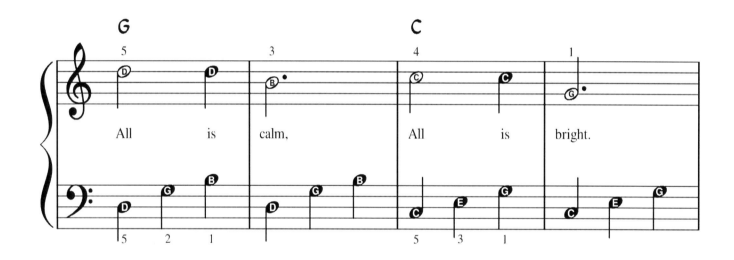

All is calm, All is bright.

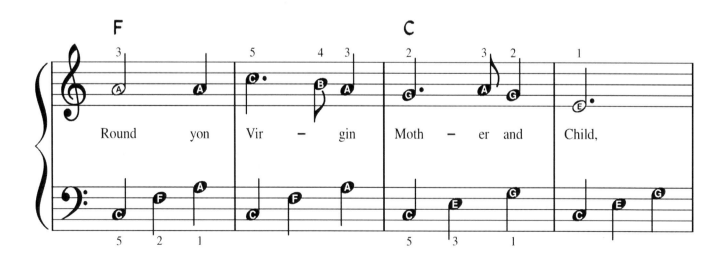

Round yon Vir – gin Moth – er and Child,

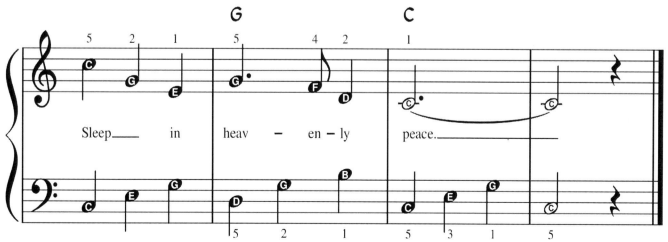

Oranges And Lemons

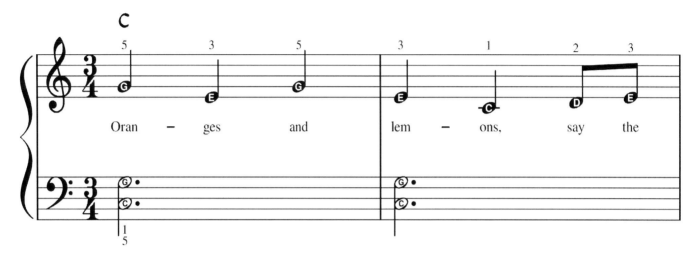

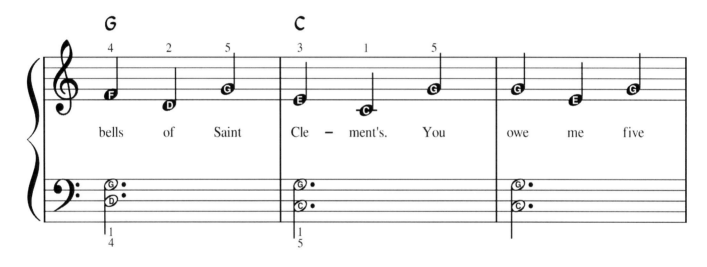

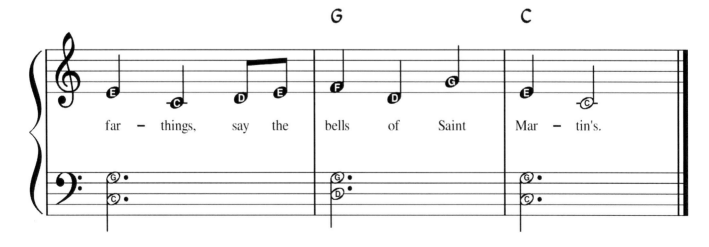

Ring a Ring o' Roses

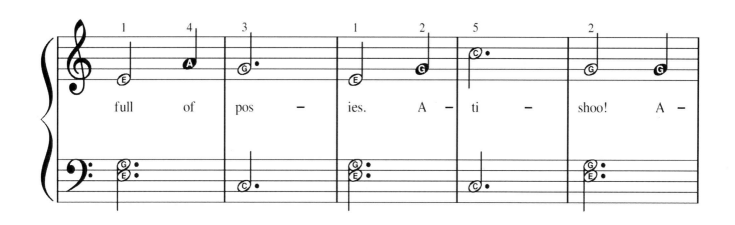

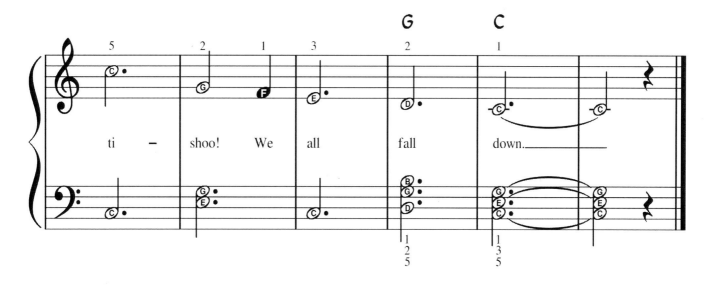

Oh! Susanna

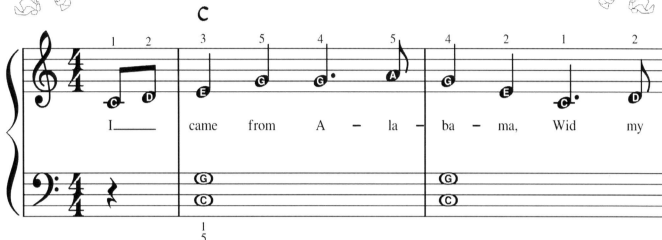

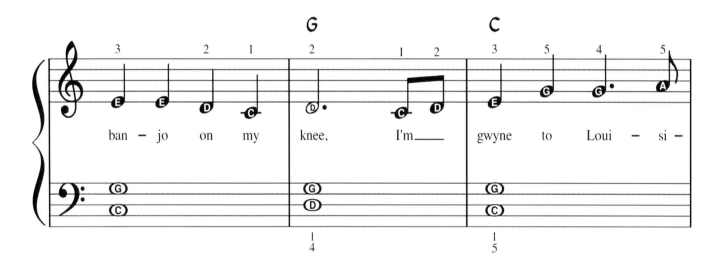

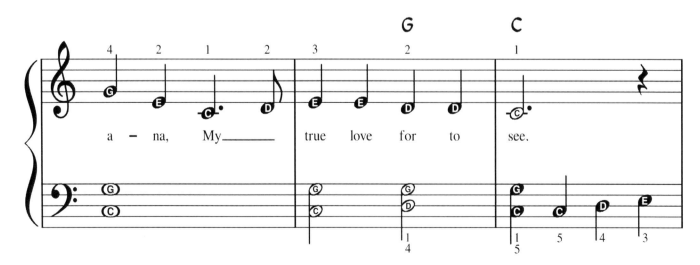

Drunken Sailor

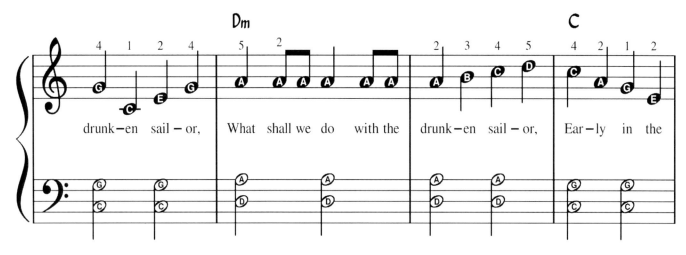

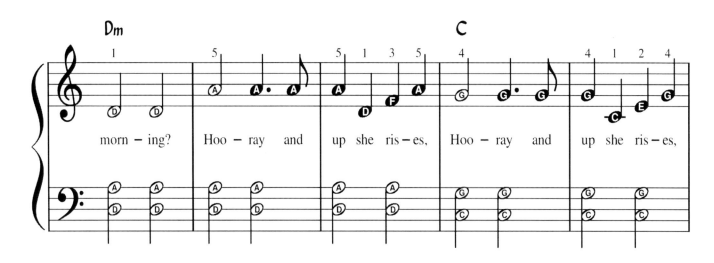

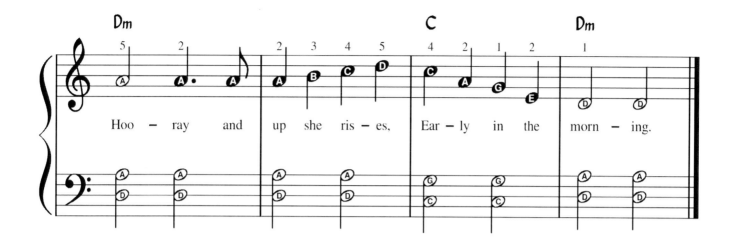

Hot Cross Buns

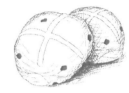

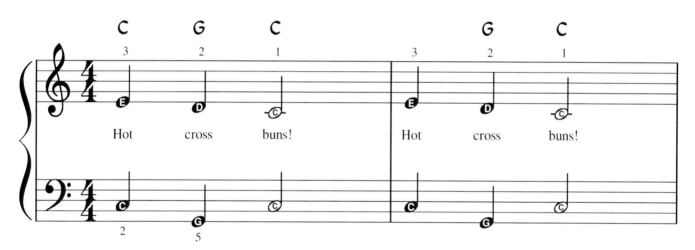

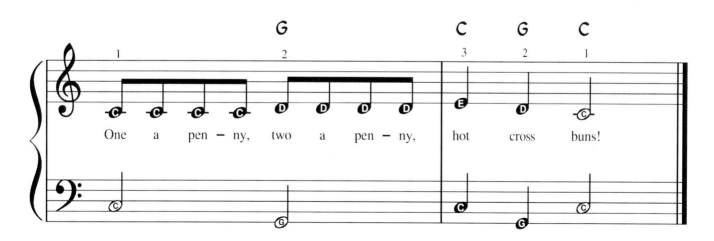

Hush, Little Baby

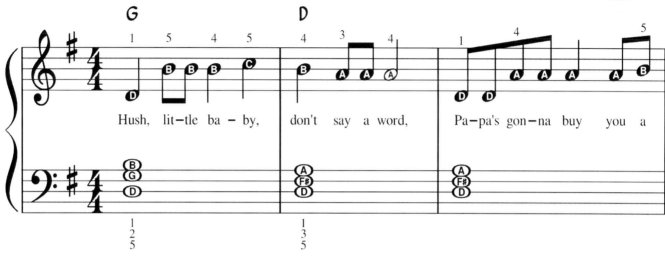

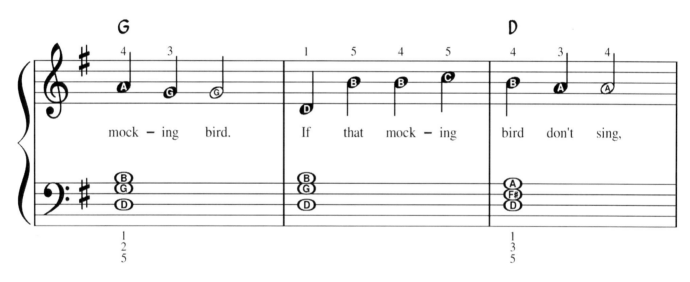

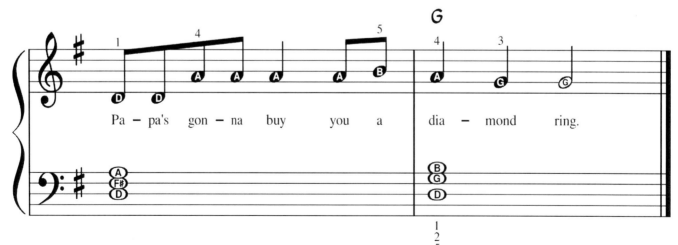

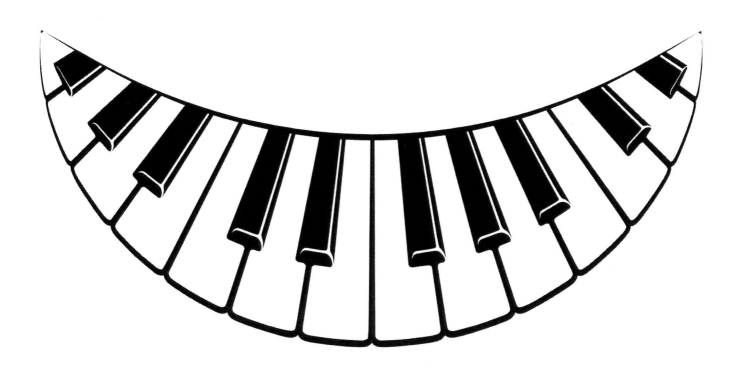

Visit us online at:
easy-sheet-music.com

Made in United States
North Haven, CT
10 December 2021

12372125R10028